Six ESSENTIALS OF SPIRITUAL AUTHENTICITY

Carol Kent & Karen Lee-Thorp

NAVPRESS
BRINGING TRUTH TO LIFE
P.O. Box 35001, Colorado Springs, Colorado 80935

OUR GUARANTEE TO YOU

We believe so strongly in the message of our books that we are making this quality guarantee to you. If for any reason you are disappointed with the content of this book, return the title page to us with your name and address and we will refund to you the list price of the book. To help us serve you better, please briefly describe why you were disappointed. Mail your refund request to: NavPress, P.O. Box 35002, Colorado Springs, CO 80935.

The Navigators is an international Christian organization. Our mission is to reach, disciple, and equip people to know Christ and to make Him known through successive generations. We envision multitudes of diverse people in the United States and every other nation who have a passionate love for Christ, live a lifestyle of sharing Christ's love, and multiply spiritual laborers among those without Christ.

NavPress is the publishing ministry of The Navigators. NavPress publications help believers learn biblical truth and apply what they learn to their lives and ministries. Our mission is to stimulate spiritual formation among our readers.

Cover photo by Bill Miles / The Stock Market
Cover design by Jennifer Mahalik
Creative Team: Amy Spencer, Terry Behimer, Vickie Howard

Some of the anecdotal illustrations in this book are true to life and are included with the permission of the persons involved. All other illustrations are composites of real situations, and any resemblance to people living or dead is coincidental.

Unless otherwise identified, all Scripture quotations in this publication are taken from the *HOLY BIBLE: NEW INTERNATIONAL VERSION* ® (NIV®) Copyright © 1973, 1978, 1984 by International Bible Society. Used by permission of Zondervan Publishing House. All rights reserved. Other version used: the *King James Version* (KJV).

Printed in the United States of America

2 3 4 5 6 7 8 9 10 11 12 13 14 15 / 05 04 03 02

CONTENTS

INTRODUCTION

Wanted:
Real Christian Women

REMEMBER the first time you read *The Velveteen Rabbit?* On Christmas morning, Rabbit was a brand-new gift, stuffed inside Boy's stocking. At night, when the nursery magic began, the toys began talking to each other. Many of the expensive toys snubbed Rabbit, but the wise old Skin Horse was kind to him.

One day Rabbit asked his friend, Skin Horse, "What is Real?" Skin Horse replied thoughtfully, "Real isn't how you are made. . . . It's a thing that happens to you. When a child loves you for a long, long time, not just to play with, but REALLY loves you, then you become Real."

Rabbit asked if it hurt to become Real. Skin Horse responded, "Sometimes. . . . Becoming Real doesn't often happen to those who break easily or have sharp edges or have to be carefully kept." Step by step, Skin Horse had learned to feel secure in the transforming love of his master, knowing he was designed for this role. [1]

In many ways, it's the same for Christians. We become authentic in our spirituality when we fully receive and embrace the love of the Father and when we model the authentic example of Jesus Christ, knowing *we were designed for this role.* In an age of image and spin, being real is prized. Few of us want to be fake. We long to be, during the week, the people we sing about being on Sunday. But *how* do we become spiritually authentic or real?

An authentic person, says the dictionary, is genuine—worthy of trust or reliance. To be spiritually authentic is to have a genuine spiritual life. To be tuned in to the real God, not one we've made up to make us feel good. To actually live by the beliefs that come out of our mouths at church. To be the same person in private that we are in public. Authenticity is the opposite of faking it. It's being the person God created us to be.

One of the chief reasons people give for not going to church is that they don't like the hypocrites. Interestingly, the earliest recorded instance of someone using the Greek word *hypokrites* to describe a person who is religious on the outside but self-centered on the inside is in the Gospels. Jesus said it first. In Greek, a *hypokrites* was simply an actor. Perhaps Jesus observed the crowds flocking to the huge theater in Sepphoris, near His hometown of Nazareth. He watched the actors perform in their brightly painted masks, as was traditional in Greek theater. And it struck Him that religious people are too often like actors, performing roles and hiding their true selves behind masks.

None of us wants to be a *hypokrites*, an actor. But maybe nobody has ever explained exactly how to become the real thing. This study offers you six steps that will take you far down the road toward becoming spiritually authentic. Using the life of Christ as our model, we'll face issues and choices that will help us own up to our acting and to define time in the measurement of eternity. We'll study the habits Jesus practiced and get an inside view of the value of God's kingdom.

The topics we'll cover aren't the only steps on the road, but they are six of the big ones. And they're not paint-by-numbers exercises. You won't become authentic in six weeks, but if you devote yourself to these habits, they will change your life. Once a "velveteen woman" fully experiences the transforming love of her Master, she becomes a *really* authentic Christian. Guaranteed.

How to Use This Guide

You were born to be a woman of influence. No—we don't mean a busybody or a queen bee, telling others what to do or making their lives revolve around yours. You were born to model your life on Jesus' life, and in so doing, be a model for others. Perhaps your influence will happen in a few quiet words over coffee, in a hug or a prayer. Don't say, "Not me—I'm barely treading water!" If you have the Spirit of God in your life, you have what it takes. God wants to influence people through you.

We've created these *Designed for Influence* Bible studies to draw out this loving, serving, celebrating side of you. You can use this study guide in your private time with God, but you'll gain even more from it if you meet with a small group of other women who share your desire to grow and give. The study is designed around the seven life-changing principles explored in Carol Kent's book, *Becoming a Woman of Influence*. These principles, which underlay Jesus' style of influencing others, are:

- Time alone with God
- Walking and talking
- Storytelling
- Asking questions
- Compassion
- Unconditional love
- Casting vision

Each of the six sessions in this guide contains these seven sections:

An Opening Story. When you see the word "I" in this guide, you're hearing from Carol. She begins each session with a story from her own life to let you know we're not making this stuff up in some spiritual hothouse; we care about these issues because we're living them. As you read these stories, look for a point of connection between your life and Carol's.

Connecting. Next comes your chance to tell your own story about the topic at hand. If you're studying on your own, take a few minutes to write down a piece of your life story in response to the questions in this section. If you're meeting with a group, tell your stories to each other. Nothing brings a group of women together like sharing stories. It's not necessary for each person to answer every question in the rest of the study, but each person should have a chance to respond to the "Connecting" questions. Sharing stories is great fun, but try to keep your answers brief so that you'll have time for the rest of the study!

Learning from the Master. The entire Bible is the Word of God. Yet Jesus Himself is the Word of God made flesh. The Bible studies in this series focus on Jesus' words and actions in the Gospels. You'll get to see how Jesus Himself grappled with situations much like those you face. He's the smartest guy in history, the closest to the Father, the one who understood life better than anyone else. This is your opportunity to follow Him around and watch how He did it. If you're meeting with a group, you don't need to answer the questions ahead of time, but it would be helpful to read through them and begin thinking about them. When your group gathers, ask for one or more volunteers to read the Scripture aloud. If the story is lengthy, you could take turns reading paragraphs. Or if you really want to have fun, assign the roles of Jesus and the other characters to different readers. Karen wrote the Bible study section of this guide, and if you have any questions or comments, you can e-mail her at bible.study@navpress.com.

A Reflection. This section contains some thoughts on the topic as well as some questions that invite you to apply what you've learned to your own life. If you're meeting with a group, it is helpful, but not necessary, to read the reflection ahead of time. When your group reaches this point in the study, you can allow people a few minutes to read over the reflection to refresh their memories. Talk about the ideas in this section that seem especially helpful to you.

Talking with God. This section closes your meeting if you're studying with a group. Inviting God to enable you to live what you've discussed may be the most important thing you do together. In addition to the prayer ideas suggested in this section, feel free to include your personal concerns.

Time Alone with God. This section and the next are your "homework" if you are meeting with a group. The first part of your "homework" is to take some time during the week to be with God. In this section you'll find ideas for prayer, journaling, thinking, or just *being* with God. If you're already accustomed to taking time away from the rush of life to reflect and pray, then you know how these quiet moments energize you for the rest of your week. If you've believed yourself to be "too busy" to take this time to nourish your hungry soul, then this is your chance to taste the feast God has prepared for you.

Walking with Others. The second part of your "homework" is to pass on God's love to someone else in some way. Here you'll sample what it means to be a woman of influence simply by giving away something you've received. This is your chance to practice compassion, unconditional love, and vision-casting with the women you encounter in your daily life.

That's how the Christian life works: we draw apart to be with God, then we go back into the world to love as we have been loved.

If you're meeting with a group, one woman will need to take responsibility for facilitating the discussion at each meeting. You can rotate this responsibility or let the same person facilitate all six sessions. The facilitator's main task is to keep the discussion moving forward and to make sure everyone has a chance to speak. This will be easiest if you limit the size of your discussion group to no more than eight people. If your group is larger than eight (especially in a Sunday school class), consider dividing into subgroups of four to six people for your discussion.

Spiritual influence is not just for super-Christians. You can make a difference in someone's life by letting God work through you. Take a chance—the results may surprise you!

1

DEVELOP A PASSION FOR JESUS

How do we fall more deeply in love with Christ?
The same way we fall in love with a person. . . .
Friendship and love develop from spending time
together, talking, and doing pleasurable things
together.

—CAROLE MAYHALL[1]

WELL into my second year of marriage, I was overwhelmed with
how *often* the laundry had to be done and how much effort it took
to keep a house clean. My husband was still finishing up school and
I was teaching. Gene and I were also the youth directors at our
church and organized all of the special events for grades seven
through twelve. I was not only *busy*. I was *tired!*

I had known Jesus from childhood and had developed the daily
habit of spending time alone with Him. But these days, something
was missing from my quiet time. Sometimes after reading the same

chapter in the Bible twice, I *still* didn't remember anything about what I'd read. When I prayed, my mind wandered to things like ungraded book reports or the sink full of dirty dishes. Even more troubling was my lack of joy. Bible reading and prayer seemed like an *obligation,* not an *opportunity* to spend time with my best Friend. My life was busy with good things—*spiritual things*—but the passion I once had for Jesus wasn't there.

Then one day I was in the home of Granny Gruenberg, the teacher of the junior high Sunday school class. As we prepared the food for a youth event, I noticed the peaceful expression on Granny's face. "How do you keep your joy, Granny?" I asked.

Granny came around the table to put her arm around me. "Carol," she said, "you're making too much *work* out of it. You just need to let Jesus love you, and then you love Him right back. *Just enjoy His presence.*" Granny told me she talked to the Lord about everything. Her day was an ongoing conversation with Him. She said, "As I've been setting this table, I've been praying for the young man or woman who will be sitting at this table in another hour. When my doorbell rings, I talk to the Lord about who is on the other side of that door. When the telephone rings, I'm praying for the person I'm talking to. When I read God's Word, I first ask Him to open my heart to the truth I'm about to read. Then after I read, I write a love letter to Jesus. He's my best friend and I love to tell Him how I responded to what He told me through His Word. But the biggest part of my joy comes when I praise Him!"

That day was a turning point. My time with God became an appointment with my dearest Friend. I started practicing silent con-versational prayer—praying for a student in the hallway at school, praying for the girl from the youth group who phoned me. I used my drive to school to verbalize my love for Jesus *out loud*. I played praise music in my car and sang at the top of my lungs. I started reading God's Word as if it were a love letter to me. When I began to practice an ongoing sense of God's presence, I felt a renewed passion for Jesus. I sensed His joy.

Authentic Christianity begins with a personal encounter with Jesus Christ. But passion for Jesus stays alive when we put meaningful time into the relationship, enjoying His presence. Sometimes we experience a dryness in our soul when we've prayed the sinner's prayer, but we're not deeply aware of how much we've been forgiven and how much He loves us. At other times we're so busy *doing things for Him* that we forget He wants us to *be with Him*. In this session we'll see how a notoriously sinful woman made the first move toward spiritual authenticity when she expressed passion for Jesus. We'll think about why a passion for Jesus is so essential for an authentic spiritual life.

1. Think back to when you first became interested in Jesus, however long ago or recently that was. What was going on in your life at the time? What attracted your attention to Jesus?

Some of us began our relationships with Christ as a legal transaction: We accepted the fact that Jesus died for our sins, and so His right standing with the Father was legally accounted to us. We may have heard a great deal about having "a personal relationship with Jesus," but we've ended up having a formal acquaintance rather than a passionate love for this most extraordinary man.

The key to having the kind of spiritual life we were meant to have is to make that "personal relationship" a reality that we experience daily, hourly, moment by moment. Jesus' earliest disciples began to follow Him around because He fascinated them. They were convinced He had what they were looking for. He *was* what they were looking for. And the more time they spent with Him, the more fascinated they were. We can read almost anywhere in the Gospels and catch their excitement.

2. Read Luke 7:36-50. Picture this scene: You're at a dinner party hosted by a devout man. The guest of honor is a famous Bible teacher. The home is a large place in which people come and go, and because there is no security system, it's not difficult for a woman of ill repute to gain access. In front of everyone, she does what the first paragraph of this story describes. What is going through your mind . . .

about the woman?

about the famous teacher?

3. How does Jesus respond to the woman's expression of feelings?

4. To explain His response, Jesus tells a story (Luke 7:41-42). What's the point of His story?

5. What do Jesus' words and actions in this scene tell you about Him as a person? How do you see Him, based on this incident?

6. Now imagine yourself in the woman's place. You own an alabaster jar of perfumed ointment—a fabulously expensive and beautiful object. In order to use the perfume, you will have to break the jar because it is carved stone without a stopper. What would it take for you to smash and use this prized possession in a public demonstration of passion for someone? (Remember: This is not taking place in a church or retreat setting, where expressing emotion for

Jesus is approved of. This is taking place in front of people who will think you are either crazy or morally debased.)

7. Why did this woman publicly humiliate herself like this? What could it have been about Jesus that so moved her?

> *To know and feel God's love is to know the deep kind of abiding joy that you want to splash all over others.*
>
> —BARBARA JOHNSON [2]

Developing a Passion for Jesus
Recently I had lunch with a group of Christian friends who don't see each other very often. Part of our time was spent "doing lunch," as girlfriends do, with exuberant chatter and updates on recent events and family transitions. But the last part of the visit was a time of revealing our hearts.

It was Michelle's turn to talk. Most of us had taken too much time to share, but Michelle surprised me. With a reflective look in her eyes she said, "I just want to live my life to make Jesus smile." That was it. Plain and simple.

After the lunch, I realized that was the most profound statement that had been made. *Living to make Jesus smile.* What did it mean? What should it mean to *me?* If I have a passion for Jesus, one of my highest goals will be to make Him smile. Here are three ways we can develop a passion for Him:

- *Get to know Him personally.* Understanding the difference between knowing *about* someone and knowing someone *personally* is essential. The Christian life begins with a one-on-one encounter with Jesus. (If you aren't sure what that means, ask your small-group leader to explain it.)
- *Hang out with Him.* The greatest honor a friend bestows on me is the gift of time. When someone cares for me enough to *want* to be with me, it makes me feel valued. I started to fall more deeply in love with Jesus when I began reading His Word every day. Then, as I meditated on what I read (His voice to me), I started having ongoing conversations with Him in prayer throughout the day.
- *Make His priorities your priorities.* We become like the person we are passionate about—Jesus. When we live to make Jesus smile, what's important to Him becomes highly important to us. Some of our similar passions might be making truth known, caring for the broken-hearted, challenging people to move beyond their limitations, spending time with unlovely people, feeding the hungry, caring for children, and helping people to understand important principles through stories and key questions. What are some practical ways you could live out His priorities this week?

> *Let my heart be broken by things that break the heart of God.*
>
> —BOB PIERCE, FOUNDER, WORLD VISION[3]

8. How passionate are you about Jesus these days? What feeds or hinders your passion?

9. What do you think about the ideas suggested in this session for cultivating a passion for Jesus? Which, if any, seem relevant to your life?

If you're meeting with a small group, take a few minutes to tell Jesus why you're passionate about Him. (If you're not passionate, go ahead and tell Him why. He'll meet you where you are.) Give each woman a chance to say at least one sentence aloud.

It will be important that those in the group who are naturally more emotive and talkative not overwhelm those for whom "passion" is less flamboyant, as well as those who may feel they're in a spiritual dry spell. Make space in your prayer time for each person, in whatever state she finds herself.

It's hard to develop a passion for Jesus if you spend time with Him only in snatched moments throughout the week. Passion for anyone grows in leisurely time spent together. Unfortunately, leisurely time is rare today. So decide this week to ignore television and magazines in order to curl up with a Good Book. Spend at least an hour reading the gospel of John. Read it as though it's a novel you've never read before. Watch the character of Jesus. Notice what He says and does. Notice how people respond to Him. What impresses you about Him? Is He worth the kind of wild love expressed by the woman in Luke 7?

Tell someone that you're learning about passion for Jesus. You could tell a new Christian—ask her if she's passionate about Jesus, and if so, what fuels that excitement. You could tell someone who has been a Christian for a while—tell her what the woman in Luke 7 did at the dinner party, and ask her what she thinks about behavior like that. You could tell someone who doesn't know Jesus at all—don't use a lot of syrupy religious language, just tell her about the story in Luke 7 and the crazy way Jesus and the woman behaved.

> *Instead of focusing on the boundaries, Jesus focused on the center, the heart of spiritual life. . . . He named a fundamentally different way of identifying who are the children of God: Do they love God, and do they love the people who mean so much to him?*
>
> —JOHN ORTBERG[4]

2

RECOGNIZE THE UNPARALLELED VALUE OF GOD'S KINGDOM

*The presence of God in a believer's life makes every-
thing spiritual. When eternity dwells within you,
your life is not ordinary because you house the Lord
of Glory. Each moment, no matter how mundane,
is infused with eternal spiritual significance.*

—MIMI WILSON AND SHELLY COOK VOLKHARDT [1]

THE guest speaker was a missionary from the Baja Peninsula of
Mexico. During the entire presentation I sensed God's anointing
on this man. His selfless lifestyle and Christlike attitude were even
more powerful than his spoken message. As he spoke of the urgent
need for people to do short-term mission work, my husband and
I glanced at each other and knew what we were both thinking.

We had saved enough money for a "comfy" family vacation, but it was just enough for plane tickets and our room and board for this summer mission project. It meant giving up our plans, but we knew the mission trip would provide valuable memories. On that trip we dealt with crowded sleeping conditions, roach-infested lodging, heat and humidity, an absence of electricity, and beans, beans, and *more* beans for every meal. There were moments when the memory of what I had relinquished in order to go crowded out my original perspective of participating in God's plan.

One day I taught a Bible study (with the help of an interpreter) to a group of women gathered at the church. These women hung on every word and didn't want to leave when it was over. Their love for Jesus and their hunger for biblical teaching made me weep. I wanted a shower, clean clothes, fresh sheets, and air conditioning. They wanted more of Him. God's kingdom work was obvious in this place, yet I rebelled against aligning my heart to what He wanted to do through me, because it meant sacrificing personal comfort and touching people who were dirty and smelly. I was sick of the beans. I was sick of the smells. I was sick of the roaches. I hated being there and counted the days until I could return home. I went back to my room and sobbed.

The senior missionary put an arm around me. "Carol," she said, "pray that God will help you love these people. When you love the people, you'll be able to fit in with what God is doing here." After one more miserable day, I was able to confess my arrogant, disobedient, selfish attitude to God. I told Him how prideful I had been. I asked Him to help me to love these people and to position my heart to match up with His plans.

To my surprise, everything about the experience started changing. The first thing I noticed was an ability to breathe the stagnant air without gagging. I began to see the hurts in the eyes of the women, and I held them and their babies in my arms. I watched them listen eagerly to the Bible teaching. I knew God wanted me to financially support what He was doing in this place. I also realized that what I thought was a personal sacrifice was actually the *privilege* of being a citizen of God's kingdom. With difficulty, I was learning that participating in God's kingdom means *doing what the King wants done.* In this session we'll look at a story Jesus told about God's kingdom and ask ourselves, "Why should we value the kingdom so much?"

1. If your house was on fire and you had time to rescue one item (other than family members or pets), what would it be?

When we are passionate about Jesus, we care about the things that spark His passion. The number one thing Jesus talked about during His earthly ministry was the kingdom of God, or the kingdom of heaven. His whole message could be summed up in the announcement: "Repent, for the kingdom of heaven is near" (Matthew 4:17). He often told stories about the kingdom of heaven, stories designed to provoke thought and response rather than just to convey dry information.

2. Read Matthew 13:44. What do you think Jesus wants us to realize about the kingdom when He compares it to a "treasure hidden in a field"?

3. How does the man who discovers this treasure respond? What are his emotions? His actions?

4. What is Jesus' point here? How does He want us to respond when we discover the kingdom?

Many of us have only the vaguest notion of *what* the kingdom of God *is,* so it's not surprising that we have difficulty treating it like the most precious thing we've ever found. Just what is it?

Dallas Willard explains that God's kingdom "is the range of his effective will, where what he wants done is done." Everything that obeys God, "whether by nature or by choice, is *within* his kingdom." The stars and planets, black holes and supernovas, are within God's kingdom because they obey His laws of physics by nature. The angels are within God's kingdom because they obey God's will by choice. Individual human hearts, along with collective social and political institutions run by humans, are "the only place in all of creation where the kingdom of God, or his effective will, is currently permitted to be absent."[2]

So the kingdom of God is not primarily inside our hearts. It is primarily *everywhere else,* and we have to choose, through faith and commitment to Christ, to move our hearts into God's kingdom. Likewise, we have to choose as families or communities to move those families or communities into God's kingdom. God forces no one; until the end of this age, an individual, a family, or a nation is free to choose whether or not to join God's kingdom.

5. Think about the realm where what God wants done is done. You might think about the solar system or the oceans—or a family where the family members are deeply invested in getting done what God wants done. What is good or beautiful about such a place?

6. Read Psalm 145. It is a song in praise of the King and His kingdom. As you read, write down everything you observe about the beauty or goodness of . . .

God

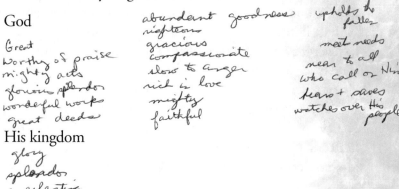

Great
Worthy of praise
mighty acts
glorious splendor
wonderful works
great deeds

abundant goodness
righteous
gracious
compassionate
slow to anger
rich in love
mighty
faithful

upholds the fallen
meet needs
near to all who call on Him
hears + saves
watches over His people

His kingdom

glory
splendor
everlasting

If you're meeting with a group, share your observations with the group.

7. Now go back to Matthew 13:44. Why should we view the kingdom as such a treasure?

8. What would it look like, in practice, to sell everything you have to buy the field with that treasure?

Being part of the kingdom means doing what the King wants done. It means obedience. Some of us view obedience as a hard, heavy thing. That might be true if the King were not so good and beautiful. How different it is to think, *I'm so lucky to have a chance to obey this King!*

9. What are some of the things that hinder us from going wild with joy over the kingdom and from spending whatever it takes to be part of the kingdom?

Doing What the King Wants Done

The key to experiencing the joy of *living* and *thriving* in God's kingdom is obedience. Here are some keys to living as a child of God's kingdom:

- *Experience intimacy with God.* As we develop an intimate love relationship with Him, God reveals His secrets to us. Psalm 25:14 (KJV) tells us, "The secret of the LORD is with those who fear Him, and He will show them His covenant." In other words, God "confides" in us when we hold Him in the place of highest honor. This intimacy helps us view the world and people in the world from His perspective. God is much more interested in a love relationship with us than in what we can *do* for Him.
- *Align your will with His will.* We learn how to obey God by joining Him where He is already at work and fitting in with what He wants to accomplish in His kingdom. Where do you see God at work in the world around you? Where does He invite you to participate (not take charge or watch passively)?
- *Settle the issue of God's trustworthiness.* When we have an intimate relationship with Him and actively align our

will with His will, we agree to follow Him, even if He doesn't reveal all of the details of the adventure. This total allegiance assumes that the trust issue is settled. As long as we're doubting God's trustworthiness, we're still unsure whether the treasure in the field is priceless or not. For some of us, settling this trust issue takes time. If that's true for you, move it to the top of your agenda. Do you believe you've struck gold, or are you too unsure to bet everything you have?

- *Verbalize your willingness to participate in His kingdom.* In a simple prayer, tell Him you want to follow Jesus' example, doing what the King wants done. Pledge your total surrender and obedience to do anything He asks you to be involved in.

- *Expect results.* When your intimacy leads to an action step of aligning your plans with His plans, your obedience will produce results in the kingdom of God. Henry Blackaby says, "Not only do *you* experience God's power and presence, but *so do those who observe what you are doing.*" [3] Your obedience becomes a catalyst for motivating more Christians to become part of fulfilling the master plan He has for His kingdom.

That's an exciting way to live—*doing what the King wants done!* Are you ready to join the adventure?

10. On your own, write down three places where you have recently seen God at work.

11. Pick one of those places and write down one way you could align your will with His and join Him where He is already at work.

12. Where are you on the question of trust? How convinced are you that you've struck gold? If you have lingering doubts, what's your plan for addressing them?

> There is a way of ordering our mental life on more than one level at once. On one level we may be thinking, discussing, seeing, calculating, meeting all the demands of external affairs. But deep within, behind the scenes, at a profounder level, we may also be in prayer and adoration, song and worship and a gentle receptiveness to divine breathings.
>
> —THOMAS KELLY[4]

To begin your prayer time, read Psalm 145 aloud. You could read in unison. Or, divide into two groups, and let one group read the even-numbered verses while the other group reads the odd-numbered verses. When you are finished, allow an open time of prayer when group members can talk to God about the areas of their lives in which they feel called to participate in God's kingdom through obedience.

Afterward, write your name on a small piece of paper. Put all the names in a bowl, and let everyone draw a name. Be sure you don't have your own name. The person whose name you draw is the person for whom you are praying this week. See "Walking with Others" on the next page.

What do you think about obedience, honestly? If you're not passionate about the King, if you don't think He's the most good and beautiful and wise King you could possibly have, then obedience could feel suffocating. Write a letter to God, telling Him exactly what you think about following Him as your King. Are you in a specific situation where you have a chance to act as a citizen of the kingdom? If so, write about that.

When you're done, read what you've written. Did you write more about the *cost* of obedience or about the *value* of the King you're obeying?

As early in the week as possible, make contact with the woman for whom you are praying. You could catch her right after your meeting or phone her later. Ask her about an area where she's currently being challenged to obey God. Ask her what *value* she sees in acting as a kingdom citizen in this situation. Ask her how you can pray for her.

> *The question before us is what the Christian life, true spirituality, really is, and how it may be lived in a [twenty-first] century setting.*
>
> —FRANCIS SCHAEFFER[5]

3

Cultivate Honesty About Sin and Limitations

Many Christians are unthinkably horrified when a real sinner is suddenly discovered among the righteous. So we remain alone with our sin, living in lies and hypocrisy. . . . He who is alone with his sins is utterly alone.

—Dietrich Bonhoeffer [1]

When our son graduated from the U.S. Naval Academy, his first assignment was a year-long engineering school in Orlando, Florida. He quickly found a church home with a superb singles program. It was an answer to his parents' prayers that he was surrounding himself with Christian friends and participating in a weekly Bible study.

As spring turned into summer, we learned he had made several very close friends in his Bible study, including April, a young woman with two little girls, Chelsea (age six) and Hannah (age three). I found myself with a lump in my throat when Jason said he was seriously attracted to April and wanted Gene and me to come to Florida to meet her. I was convinced we could talk him out of this unwise relationship.

In mid-August, Gene and I were in Denver. We called home for our messages and our son's voice greeted us on the answering machine. "Mom and Dad, some things are comin' down. We have to talk!" That was it. For hours we tried to reach him, but there was no answer. Tension mounted. When we finally connected, he said, "My naval orders have changed. I have to report to Surface Warfare Officers' School in Newport, Rhode Island, on September 8. April and I are in love, and we want to get married next Friday."

My heart felt like it fell out of my body. I was hyperventilating. My husband took over the conversation while I regained my composure. My son was not only telling us he wanted to marry a woman we had never met—he was telling us he wanted to marry a divorced woman with two children! This was *not* on my list of expectations. I had prayed for a virgin, and this woman didn't qualify! However, their minds were made up and I instinctively knew we could cause a breach in our relationship that would last a lifetime, or we could get on board and help with the wedding. We talked them into waiting three weeks.

I sobbed until I thought my heart would break. How could this be God's will? I could hardly bring myself to tell family and friends that they were invited to a wedding. For days I struggled with my emotions, never realizing it was my own sin of pride that was the root of my problem. My self-deception was easy to nurse, and I positioned my heart to be unhappy about my son's choice of a wife.

Two weeks later Jason and April walked into our home arm-in-arm. Chelsea and Hannah were close behind. Within a half-hour,

Chelsea came running up and took my hand in her two hands. With her big brown eyes gleaming, she squealed, "You're my new, favorite Grammy." My heart was melting. Hannah tilted her head and grinned. "I love you, too, Grammy." I soon heard the details of April's challenging testimony and realized what a godly young woman she was. I had been so wrong about her. On my knees I told God how sorry I was for being so full of the sin of pride.

Sometimes we fail to see our own hypocrisy as sin, or we rationalize that it's not really a *big* problem. We can make up excuses and defenses for all kinds of sin, from a "little" lie to big games with money or people's hearts. In this session we'll look at another of Jesus' stories to see why honesty about our sin is so crucial. You will need paper and pens for this session.

1. Which of the following best describes your reputation when you were a child?

   □ *The good child:* I rarely got into trouble. Such a little angel!
   □ *The problem child:* I often got into trouble. I was no angel!
   □ *The invisible child:* Nobody paid enough attention to me to notice whether I was into trouble.
   □ *The entertaining child:* I was a handful, but I was so charming or funny that people didn't mind so much.

It's easy to get the mistaken notion that being Christian means playing the good child. If being the good child comes naturally to us, it's doubly easy. We've seen how important obedience is to the authentic spiritual life. Doesn't that mean God wants us to be good little girls who follow all the rules?

Jesus lived in a religious climate where good little girls and boys were praised, and bad girls and boys were shunned. About the worst thing you could be was a tax collector. Tax collectors were Jews who won contracts from the Roman government to collect the taxes for a given area. They agreed to pay a certain sum to the government, and anything above it that they could extort through intimidation was theirs to keep. Thus, not only were they collaborating with the hated Romans, but they were also little better than gangsters in their tactics. No decent Jew would have anything to do with them.

Pharisees, on the other hand, were members of a highly regarded religious party. They were known to be the most committed to God, the most obedient, and the most respectable people around. Even people who couldn't imagine living up to their standards admired them.

2. Read Luke 18:9-14. To whom did Jesus address this parable?

3. Jesus often designed His parables to turn the tables on our expectations. How does this parable do that?

4. What's wrong with the Pharisee's attitude in this story?

5. It's possible to pretend to be like the tax collector. We can beat our breasts and say, "God, have mercy on me, a sinner," without really facing the actual, specific sin in our lives. How can you tell the difference between pretend confession and genuine confession?

6. Why do you think honesty about the true state of our hearts and our behavior is so important to God?

7. If honesty is so important, why do we often find it so difficult?

In Jesus' story, the Pharisee's core sin was pride, or what Jesus called exalting himself (Luke 18:14). Pride is an excessive opinion of our own qualities, abilities, or importance. Feeling secure in our worth as a human being or child of God is not pride (as long as we don't think we have more worth than other human beings). Feeling good about a job well done need not be pride either. The problem comes when feeling good about our good deeds blinds us to our omission of good in other areas.

A subtler form of pride is the belief that we should be perfect. Pride says, "It's all right for other people to sin. But I am *me*, and therefore I should never fail. I must punish myself for failing so I will never do it again. I hate having to humble myself before God and admit my weakness. I hate admitting I'm an ordinary human. Therefore I will drive myself and beat myself to do everything perfectly."

8. Which is more of a temptation for you: (a) to ignore or minimize your faults, or (b) to beat yourself up for having faults? How has that played itself out recently? (If you've conquered both of these errors, perhaps you can share with the group how you did it!)

Searching for Truth, Defining Honesty

Several years ago I was on a panel of Christian leaders and professors at an education convention. A student in the audience
asked me, "What is the difference between absolute and relative
truth?" It sounded like a trick question, but then it occurred to
me that in our postmodern world people want to believe that
whatever is truth to them is okay—that there is no absolute standard. Our children are being taught this way of thinking as if it
is a fact of life. In a world without an absolute standard of truth,
being honest can become subjective.

George Barna asked the following question in a recent poll:
"Do you agree or disagree with this statement: There is no such
thing as absolute truth. People can define truth in different ways
and still be correct." Twenty-eight percent of those polled
strongly agreed that there is no such thing as absolute truth.
Another 38 percent somewhat agreed, meaning 66 percent of
Americans do not believe in absolutes.[2]

As a Christian, I *do* believe in absolute truth, and I long to
learn how to cultivate honesty with God, with others, and with
myself. Here's a checklist of ten questions that help me get rid
of my pride and peel my heart down to gut-level honesty:

- Do I try to give the impression that I'm better than I
  really am?
- Do I embellish the truth in order to make a story about
  myself or someone else more interesting?
- Did I do anything today that made my conscience feel
  uneasy?
- Am I honest in my dealings with neighbors, coworkers,
  relatives, and friends?
- Do I cheat on my taxes?
- Do I pay my bills on time?

- Was I too proud to admit my fault in a situation today?
- Did I do anything in private today that I would be embarrassed to admit to my best friend?
- Have I deceived someone by saying nothing?
- Do I defend God's absolute truth, or have I given in to the popular trend toward relative truth?

9. Ask God to put a magnifying lens on your heart. Which of the above questions make you uneasy? Which one do you wish was not on the list? Is there a sin you need to confess or an apology you need to make to God or to someone else?

> *If Jesus takes such a high view of the truth and reliability of Scripture, surely we can, too . . . it only makes sense that if God created us and made the rules for living right and joyful lives, He would insure that we received a trustworthy copy of that most important message.*
>
> —LAEL ARRINGTON [3]

Take five minutes on your own to write a confession of sin to God. You can write about your pride or any other sin you are aware of. The rest of the group will not see what you write.

Place what you've written in front of you, face down or

folded up. Open your prayer time with confession of sin. The leader might begin, "Lord, You are merciful and just to those who are honest about their lives. We have sinned against You through what we have done and what we have failed to do. We have not loved You with all our hearts. We have not loved our neighbors as ourselves. Please forgive us, and lead us to live differently." Then others can pray, silently or aloud.

A centuries-old way of keeping ourselves honest is to make a habit of reviewing the past twenty-four hours, asking three questions:

- *Gratitude:* What ideas, people, or experiences came to me in the past day that I can thank God for?
- *Awareness:* Where has God been present in my life in the past day?
- *Confession:* When in the past day have I failed to choose the way of love or refused the Holy Spirit's work in me and through me?

Try this with pen and paper. Make a list of things from the past day for which you are thankful, a list of moments where you recognized God's presence, and a list of ways in which you failed to love. One or more of these lists may be very short the first time you do this, but if you practice, your awareness will grow.

WALKING WITH OTHERS

Contact a woman who has been looking to you for spiritual encouragement. Make an appointment to get together informally this week. Tell her about a time in your life when you struggled over an area of honesty, or when you questioned the absolute truth in God's Word, or when you needed to make a confession to Him, or when you just needed to *get real* with God and others. Explain how you resolved this spiritual crisis or challenge in your life. Ask her if she has ever struggled in the area of "truth in the inner heart," and find out if there's a specific way she would like you to pray for her this week.

> *The discipline of confession brings an end to pretense. God is calling into being a church that can openly confess its frail humanity and know the forgiving and empowering graces of Christ. Honesty leads to confession, and confession leads to change.*
>
> —RICHARD FOSTER[4]

4

Focus on Integrity of Heart Above Outward Behavior

Jesus' followers are those who intentionally arrange their lives around the goal of spiritual transformation — the development of a well-ordered heart. We can learn to be intentional.

— John Ortberg[1]

As a young married woman, I was eager to change the world. I truly believed that one person, sold out to God, doing her part every day to influence others for His glory, could make a positive difference. I determined that when I left this earth, it was going to matter that I had been here.

In the beginning my motives were pure. I poured my energy into my day job but passionately took on a part-time position with the Lifeline Program. In the evenings, on weekends, and for special projects I invested my time and energy in troubled girls. This organization targeted high-risk youth who were drug or alcohol addicted, or in some cases had been in trouble with the legal system. Many of them were from single-parent homes and most of them lived below the poverty level.

At first the job was exhilarating. I received names and addresses from the welfare department and made house calls on "my girls." One by one I arranged times to meet with them and had numerous opportunities to lead these young women to Christ and to disciple them in their walks with Christ. This experience produced a spiritual high that I thrived on. Soon church groups and civic clubs picked up on what I was doing, and I was invited to do programs for a wide variety of Christian and secular groups. People loved to invest in my "cause" and to hear stories of the transformed lives of these young women.

But after a while the original joy of working with young women was tarnished by my disillusionment with those who chose to return to their former lifestyles. I also discovered every church and civic group wanted "a piece of me" because the cause I represented was exciting. Eventually I was smiling on the outside, but weary of my work and tired of talking about it. I also felt unappreciated by the parent organization because I was no longer reporting the same high level of "success stories" I had in the beginning.

Initially I had equated working harder with authentic spiritual success, only to find it left me feeling unfulfilled, unhappy, abused, and struggling with feelings of failure. I lost my focus. This ministry soon became all about what *I* was accomplishing (or not accomplishing) instead of about what *God* was doing. For a while I faked joy in my position of working with the girls, but my heart ached at doing it for the wrong reasons. In this session we'll look at the importance of maintaining integrity of heart, not just an outward appearance of spiritual success.

1. What has been your experience of physical exercise? Do you like it? Hate it? Do it because it's good for you? Prefer not to think about it?

When we develop a passion for Jesus and want to obey Him as King of the kingdom, we often start by trying to conform our outward behavior to His desires. We quickly encounter a problem. It's not so easy to "Just Do It." Jesus says, "Love your enemies, do good to those who hate you, bless those who curse you, pray for those who mistreat you" (Luke 6:27-28). That's a tall order! So, we often decide to fake it until we make it. We try to appear to others and ourselves as though we love everyone. We try hard to do good to all, but we end up feeling exhausted, unappreciated, used, and discouraged.

It's as though Jesus has commanded us, "Run a mile in four minutes." It's humanly possible, but extremely difficult. Yet we set off running. And we collapse in failure. We misunderstand that He's really saying, *"Become the kind of person* who can run a mile in four minutes." Start training. Start building your heart and other muscles.

2. Read Matthew 12:33-35. What determines the quality of fruit that a tree produces?

3. How is this like the relationship between our heart and our outward behavior?

4. In Matthew 15:19, Jesus says that murder (a behavior) comes out of the heart. Based on the tree/fruit analogy, how does murder come from the heart?

5. In what way does slander (a malicious statement that hurts someone's reputation) come out of the heart?

6. The heart is the core of us, the source of our emotions, thoughts, beliefs, motives, and desires. Skim the Sermon on the Mount (Matthew 5–7). What heart issues does Jesus address in the following passages? Look especially for *emotions, desires,* and *beliefs.*

Matthew 5:21-22

Matthew 5:27-28

Matthew 5:38-48

Matthew 6:19-24

Matthew 6:25-34

Matthew 7:1-5

Matthew 7:7-12

Why was Jesus so focused on changing our deepest thoughts, beliefs, and desires? Because our deepest beliefs determine what we actually do. We worry if, at the core, we don't really believe God is taking care of our needs. And if we worry, then we are hindered from acting in love. We are angry because someone has blocked our goal, a goal we believe is more important than loving that person. And if we are furious at her, then we will be unable to love her. What we really believe (not what we *say* we believe) determines both our emotional responses and our actions.

> *BE WHO YOU IS, cause if you ain't who you is, then you is who you ain't.*
>
> —HARRY HEIN[2]

What Is a Heart of Integrity?

Any time our emphasis is on looking good to observers, we're not motivated by a deep love for God and people. Here are some of the distortions we're tempted to indulge in if we focus on outward behavior:

- *Living by a list of boundaries.* Instead of focusing on what we're not allowed to do, Jesus always focused on the heart, the center of spiritual life.
- *Becoming exclusive, proud, or judgmental.* The better we look on the outside, the more an untended heart can grow weeds of pride that hinder love.
- *Becoming inaccessible to those who most need our help and to friends who hold us accountable.* If we can't seem to find the time to be with people who deeply know us, perhaps it's because we fear being known.
- *Making ministry a heavy, distasteful, laborious task.* When ministry is a performance rather than the upwelling of a grateful heart, it becomes a burden.
- *Focusing our ministry on what we've done rather than what God is doing.* If our eyes are on a program *we've* developed or the people *we've* touched, we'll lose sight of God's agenda.

Integrity of heart is a choice, but it's also a process of learning to think as Jesus thought. Adopting Jesus' thinking leads to adopting His habits. For instance, we respond to interruptions the way Jesus did. We respond to people's physical and spiritual needs without selfish motives.

John Ortberg says, "Inauthenticity involves a preoccupation with appearing to be spiritual."[3] Integrity of heart can best be maintained by asking these questions on a regular basis:

- Am I arranging my life around activities that enable me to live out the fruit of the Spirit?
- Did I read my Bible for "extra credit" with God today or because I love Him?
- Did I do anything today for the praise of the people who observed me?
- Is the ministry I do for God a joy or a burden?
- Do I say yes to certain spiritual opportunities because of what's in it for me?
- Am I close enough to God that He helps me see the needs of other people?
- Does my heart joyfully respond to meeting those needs?
- Was my smile real today, or did I try to impress someone with my superficial happiness?
- Did I give money to my church or to a Christian organization so someone would be impressed by my generosity or because I love God and His work?
- Is there anyone I dislike or hold a grudge against? If so, what will I do about it?
- Am I fearful of what will happen if someone learns the truth about me?

7. As an example of dealing with a heart issue, take Matthew 6:19-24. There are competing *desires:* desire for "treasure in heaven" or desire for possessions. There are competing *beliefs:* either God is the provider of our deepest needs or

money is the provider of our deepest needs. What would be a game plan for shifting your desires and beliefs about possessions toward the truth in this area? How would you go about seeking change at the heart level?

> *Jesus warned His disciples, we must beware of hypocrisy—pretending to be something we aren't, acting with a mask covering our face. Hypocrisy is a terrible sign of trouble in our hearts—it waits only for the day of exposure.*
>
> —JOSEPH BAYLY[4]

Pair up with someone sitting next to you. Share with each other one heart issue you can pray about for each other.

Regather as a group. Pray aloud for your partner. (If you're not used to doing this, even one sentence counts!)

One thing we can do to change our hearts is to meditate on truth. Pondering deeply on truth can help us replace deep false beliefs with true beliefs. Start reading Matthew 5 until you come to a statement that your heart doesn't fully believe. For instance, do you really, deeply believe that those who mourn will be comforted (5:4)? Do you deeply believe yourself to be blessed beyond your wildest dreams? When you come to a statement where your heart says, *Yes, but . . .,* stop there. Close your eyes and repeat the statement over in your mind. What do you doubt? Is it really true? Why should you trust it? What memories or feelings come up to contradict Jesus' words? Take all of that to God. Repeat the truth to yourself again.

Who do you know who could use some encouragement in her walk with God? Identify someone who you don't think of as far ahead of you on the road of faith. Share with her this idea of addressing the beliefs of your heart rather than your outward behavior. Tell her the belief from Matthew 5 that you are seeking to believe more deeply. Ask her to pray for you so that you and the Holy Spirit will be partners in this work of changing your heart.

> *There is no use talking about loving God except to understand that it takes place in the inward world of our thoughts. . . . The spiritual battle, the loss or victory, is always in the thought-world.*
>
> —FRANCIS SCHAEFFER[5]

5

THINK IN TERMS OF ETERNITY, NOT TIME

Something more is coming! Everything in Scripture
points to it and everything within us cries out for it.
God's work with us is not finished in this life.

—RAY STEDMAN [1]

MUCH of my life has been lived on the thin edge of overcommit-
ment. For years I took pride in being efficient enough to add two
or three items to my to-do list that would stretch my limits so I
could accomplish more on any given day. I wished for more hours
in my day so I could get more done.

I had convinced myself my hyperactivity was "for God."
Sometimes I would scan my list at the end of the day and write
down something I had already accomplished that was not on the
list so I could experience the pleasure of drawing a line through it.

55

My friends were important to me, too, but I was spending less and less time with them so I could work on important projects and goals.

In late spring I got a call from one of my oldest and closest friends. A two-hour drive separated us, but we stayed in close contact. Terri told me she and her husband were facing a heavy decision about career transitions. She was a school principal and her husband had a private practice as a lawyer. The new opportunity would mean she would transfer from her job in a friendly suburban community to an administrative job in the inner city. The same school system would also hire her husband to work with legal challenges facing the school. The offer was worded so that either they were both hired or neither would be hired.

Terri was distraught. Her husband was ready for a major change, but she was happy where she was. I told her I would pray daily that God would give both of them the wisdom to come to an agreement on this important decision.

The summer brought vacation travel and lots of out-of-town company. Our church was in the middle of a major fund-raising campaign with meetings to attend and urgent calls to return. August came. I often prayed for Terri and John, but I didn't call to find out if they had made a decision. Terri's birthday was coming up at the end of the month, and we always got together for dinner to celebrate our birthdays.

While working down my to-do list one day I realized it was past time to set up our birthday dinner. Guilt swept over me. Terri was one of the people who had prayed for me regularly during times of urgent need over a period of several years. When I had a need, she had always followed up with a phone call or encouraging note. But in *her* need for urgent prayer about a situation that could change the next several years of her life, I hadn't even taken the time to ask if a decision had been made. I had prayed for her, but not consistently. I certainly cared, but not enough to call. There were just too many things on my list that demanded urgent attention. My confession and apology to my friend were not easy to do.

God used that recent incident to remind me of a pattern in my life. I was so busy doing *things* for God that I was neglecting *people*. As I reflected on Christ's life and realized how He made time for individual people who needed a touch or a word from Him, I realized I had been caught up in "time-thinking" rather than "eternity-thinking." I had put more value on what I accomplished within twenty-four hours than on the eternal value of time spent in prayer for a friend or time spent doing acts of kindness that would encourage her. In this session we'll look at the practical difference it makes when we focus our hopes and plans on eternity rather than time.

1. What ideas or pictures come to mind when you think of the word "eternity"?

Most of us live as slaves to time. We value ourselves and others based on productivity: how much we can get done in a finite window of time. We want immediate solutions to our problems. We dread aging and hope to live longer and longer. Love takes time, but we have too little to spare. We can't imagine sacrificing for the sake of our grandchildren, let alone for something as vague as "eternity." Jesus' attitude was entirely different.

2. Just before He gave Himself up to death, Jesus explained the view of life that motivated Him. Read John 12:24-26. How was Jesus' life like a grain of wheat?

3. Jesus wanted His followers also to treat their lives as grains of wheat. Think about the example He set. What do you think He meant when He called us to "hate" our lives in this world?

4. What would it look like for you to let your life fall into the ground and die in order to bear fruit?

Faith in eternity has produced numberless abuses in Christian history. For instance, peasants have been told they must accept oppression in this life in order to receive blessing in the next. This idea has been ridiculed as "pie in the sky when you die." Also, Christians have been accused of not caring about the earth because they expect it to be destroyed soon. Neither of these ideas shows an accurate understanding of eternity.

5. Belief in "pie in the sky when you die" leads people to sit around waiting passively for heaven. How was Jesus' behavior different?

6. What risks are involved in following Jesus' example?

7. Read Matthew 6:19-21. How does eternity-thinking, rather than time-thinking, affect the way we treat possessions?

Eternity-Thinking Versus Time-Thinking

Once we fully internalize that every human being is immortal and our choices in this life matter for eternity, it changes how we make our plans, spend our money, do our jobs, use our leisure time, and interact with people. We understand that this life is *not* all there is, and we have plenty of time for the things that really matter.

But how do we live out this important choice? Here are a few suggestions that can help us practice eternity-thinking:

- *Remind yourself.* Ask yourself multiple times a day, *If I really believe that I will live forever with a good God, how will I handle this situation?*
- *Understand that "this moment" is part of eternity.* It's no more or less important than the minutes I spend doing what feels like "important stuff." Jan Johnson says, "Developing eyes for things eternal helps us understand that even when nothing is supposedly happening, God is delighting in us and working His redemption in us. One moment is not more important than the next."[2] Having an eternal mindset includes being aware of God's presence here on earth as part of an ongoing relationship that will never end. It's stopping long enough to feel His pleasure in our worship and to delight in an awareness of His direction for our day.
- *Ask the "big" question: What would Jesus do?* How would Jesus solve this problem? How would Jesus respond to this personality? What would Jesus do with this paycheck? What would Jesus do with the next five years of my life?
- *Eliminate the quest for "things."* Everything I ever purchased as a gift for myself has gotten old, out-of-date, faded, worn out, or boring. Anne Ortlund reminds us: "If you live in the gray world of trying to combine God

and materialism, you'll become more and more earthly, self-centered, dull, flabby, bloated, insensitive, and out of touch . . . If this is the life you want—[the] life of trust and rest and richness in Christ—deliberately turn your back on the touchable, material world and concentrate on the *real* world."[3]

- *Get passionate about the one thing we can only do in our earthly lifetime.* There are three things that will last forever—God, His Word, and the eternal souls of people. Evangelism is something we can do only now, so we need to be intentional about reaching the people in our sphere of influence with the truth of the gospel. When that is a burning passion of our lives, it influences how we spend our time and money.

The closer I get to understanding how short life is, the more I want to be a person who practices an eternal response to people, things, opportunities, disappointments, and celebrations.

> *This life is only the first page of the book, not the last page.*
>
> —CORRIE TEN BOOM[4]

8. Reflect on how eternity-thinking versus time-thinking influences your decisions in various areas of your life.

If this life is all there is, then my attitude toward possessions should be . . .

If this life is all there is, then my attitude toward my career should be . . .

If this life is all there is, then my attitude toward my family should be . . .

If this life is all there is, then my attitude toward nonChristians should be . . .

If this life is all there is, then my attitude toward aging should be . . .

BUT,

If my life is eternal, then my attitude toward possessions should be . . .

If my life is eternal, then my attitude toward my career should be . . .

If my life is eternal, then my attitude toward my family should be . . .

If my life is eternal, then my attitude toward nonChristians should be . . .

If my life is eternal, then my attitude toward aging should be . . .

The great use of a life is to spend it for something that will outlast it.

—WILLIAM JAMES[5]

Pair up with one or two other people in your small group. Write down three situations you have observed in yourself where you have been more *time*-minded than *eternity*-minded. Then write down the name of one friend who does not yet know the Lord that you are willing to pray for, as long as it takes, until she comes to Christ, because personal evangelism is one thing we can do *only* in this lifetime. Take turns praying conversationally about any items on your list. It can be a time of confession as well as a time of commitment to change. End by praying for your friend who does not yet know Christ. Ask God to draw her to Himself, and tell Him you are available to participate in what He wants to do in her life.

Use John 12:24-26 for meditation. You can journal about it, pray about it, and/or mull it over in your mind until you've memorized it. Allow your thoughts and emotions to surface about allowing your life to "die" in order to bear fruit. To what death is God calling you? Do you believe in eternity enough to take that risk?

Eternity-thinking means the people around you are infinitely more important than getting tasks accomplished or things purchased. Tasks and things are temporary; people are eternal. This week, treat someone whom you don't know well as eternal. Pray for her. Look for a way to encourage her faith.

> *All that is not eternal is out of date.*
>
> —C. S. Lewis[6]

6

PRACTICE THE LIFE HABITS JESUS PRACTICED

I believe when Christ became man and lived as the Son of Man that God not only gave Jesus to us as our Savior but also as our example. Jesus became our role model, fleshing out for us how man is to live in relationship to his God.

—KAY ARTHUR[1]

SOME of the greatest influencers in my life have been people who modeled the behavior, attitudes, or disciplines of Christ. Sometimes they didn't even know I was observing them. I didn't always know them as close personal friends, but I was attracted to a quality of their Christian life that I wanted to emulate. When someone practices a life habit Jesus practiced, they show us how to be more effective Christians.

Something happened a couple of years ago that demonstrates this principle. I told this story in *Becoming a Woman of Influence:*

The host [of the television program on which I was a guest] was a remarkable woman with a doctorate in educational psychology and a warm, charismatic personality. The live telecast went well, and we both enjoyed our time in the studio together. We decided to meet later, and I invited her to join me for dinner at my hotel because I was on a ministry assignment in her hometown. She politely declined dinner but set a time for us to meet later.

During our meeting she told me she hoped she had not appeared rude when she turned down my invitation to dinner, but she was fasting and felt it would be inappropriate to meet at meal-time when she was not eating. I asked her about the purpose of the fast and discovered that this godly woman had been married to a pastor, but they were separated, and he had given absolutely no hope of reconciliation. . . . With an urgent need to know more clearly the mind of God . . . she felt led to enter an extended period of prayer and fasting. Previously in her Christian walk, she had fasted for brief periods of time and experienced tremendous spiritual power and a deeper walk with the Father during those times.

Her face was radiant as she spoke to me of this intimate encounter with God. Instead of a bitter, downtrodden woman who had been dumped by her husband, she was a model of strength, beauty, intelligence, and deep spirituality. She didn't know it, but she was teaching me about the benefit and importance of fasting. She gave me literature, encouragement, and advice on how to integrate this discipline into my own prayer life. It was an impact moment in my life. [2]

Fasting was only one of the disciplines Jesus practiced. In this session we'll look at many of the life habits He modeled, including solitude, prayer, the study of Scripture, worship, and service.

1. In this study you've looked at passion for Jesus, obedience, honesty, integrity of heart, and eternity-thinking. In which of these areas would you say you are strongest? In which would you most like to grow?

We often imagine that because He was God and because He was sinless, Jesus was effortlessly passionate about the Father, obedient to the Father, wise, powerful, loving, and fruitful. No doubt it was in some ways easier for Him than for us (although who among us has endured the focused malice of Satan to the degree Jesus did?). Nevertheless, we tend to overlook His commitment to life habits that nourish spiritual strength.

2. Read Luke 4:1-13. Jesus had just been baptized and was about to begin His public ministry. Why do you suppose He did each of the following?

He went alone into a solitary place (the desert) for an extended period of time.

He fasted from food.

When tempted, He quoted the Hebrew Bible (what we now call the Old Testament).

3. Because books had to be copied by hand, they were unbelievably expensive. Jesus could not have owned a copy of the Bible. Yet He could quote it. What do you think He might have done to learn parts of the Old Testament by heart?

4. What do you imagine Jesus did during forty days alone?

5. We don't know if Jesus got another forty days alone once He began His ministry. However, Luke tells us, "Jesus often withdrew to lonely places and prayed" (Luke 5:16). Why do you suppose He did this *often?* (You might think about the situation described in Luke 5:15.)

Jesus' life had a rhythm of outward and inward spiritual practices. He went to the synagogue regularly to worship and teach (Luke 4:14-15), and He served the sick and suffering (Luke 4:40-41; 5:15). Then He went off alone to pray (Luke 4:42; 5:16).

6. Read Luke 4:14-15,40-42 and 5:15-16. Try to imagine what Jesus' life was like. What do you think each of these contributed to His life?

His time alone in prayer

His time in public worship and service

7. What aspects of Jesus' life-pattern would you like to imitate? What appeals to you about those things?

Impacting Lives Like Jesus Did

Influence is a person's indirect power over people, events, or things, not through the exercise of physical force or formal authority, but by force of character or wisdom.[3] I was surprised one day as a friend and I were discussing the title of a book I had written, *Becoming a Woman of Influence.* She felt the title was totally inappropriate because—to her—the idea of influence had to do with "strutting your stuff," pushing your own ideas as the only correct answers, and feeling more important than someone else. I argued that she needed to understand the definition of the word more clearly.

As I have studied the life of Christ, I've realized that what He modeled and taught had nothing to do with bringing attention to Himself or putting others down. It had everything to do with being an *influential* leader who by force of character, wisdom, and example influenced others' thinking and choices. He practiced life habits that help me live an authentic Christian life so that I can impact the lives of others as He did.

Here are some questions we can ask ourselves as we seek to adopt the life habits Jesus practiced:

- *Have I learned how to meditate on Scripture?* Edith Schaeffer says, "All the day long, as I walk in fields or city streets, as I sit at the typewriter or make a bed with fresh sheets, as I converse with professors or tiny eager human beings wanting to learn . . . as I work in a lab or scrub a floor . . . I can meditate upon the Law, the Word of God, which my eyes have read or my ears have heard."[4]
- *Have I set aside a time and place for solitude?* Scheduling into our lives a time when we are alone with Him will reignite our passion for God, renew our creativity, and fill us with fresh energy for daily tasks. John Ortberg reminds

us: "Wise followers of Christ's way have always understood the necessity and benefit of solitude. . . . Solitude is
the one place where we can gain freedom from the forces
of society that will otherwise relentlessly mold us."[5]

- *How and when do I pray?* Jesus certainly prayed when He
  was in agony in the Garden of Gethsemane and when
  He was suffering on the cross, but He also spent time
  alone with His Father on a regular basis, when He was
  not in crisis. He talked to the Father before and after
  major ministry assignments, but also on ordinary days.
  His life was an ongoing conversation with His Father.
- *Do I enjoy worship and service?* Richard Foster reminds us
  that "worship is our responding to the overtures of love
  from the heart of the Father. . . . [It] is human response
  to divine initiative."[6]

*The divine priority is worship first, service second. . . . If
worship does not propel us into greater obedience, it has not
been worship.*

—RICHARD FOSTER[7]

8. As you look back over the six sessions of this study, what
   do you sense the Holy Spirit is saying to you? What will
   you take with you?

Take a few minutes on your own to think about how you would complete these two sentences:

One thing I have gained from this group is . . .

One thing I would like you to pray for me as I go forward after this study is . . .

You could jot some notes about your answers. Then use these sentences as the basis for your closing prayer.

Make plans ahead of time for a morning, afternoon, or evening during the next week when you will enjoy some solitude. You'll need at least a couple of hours. You might consider trading baby-sitting times with another woman in your small group if you both have young children.

Don't feel the need to overschedule what you'll do during this time. The tone should be relaxing, not driven. You could meditate on Scripture you read earlier in the week. You could sing songs of praise and worship. (Even if you're not a singer, your voice will be beautiful to God!) Talk to God, beginning with a time of praise for His attributes, character, and creation. Voice your thanks for what He has done in your life. Tell Him your current concerns.

After taking at least the first hour to rest in God, you might reflect on which of the following habits of Jesus are weak links in your personal spiritual journey: solitude, prayer, fasting, Bible study, worship, and service. Write out one goal you have in one of those spiritual disciplines. Ask God to help you to follow through on your commitment.

Remember: Jesus doesn't drive sheep, He leads them!

If you want to learn more about the life habits Jesus practiced, here are some books to start with:

John Ortberg, *The Life You've Always Wanted* (Grand Rapids, MI: Zondervan, 1997).

Donald S. Whitney, *Spiritual Disciplines for the Christian Life* (Colorado Springs, CO: NavPress, 1991).

Bruce Demarest, *Satisfy Your Soul* (Colorado Springs, CO: NavPress, 1999).

Richard Foster, *Celebration of Discipline* (San Francisco, CA: HarperCollins, 1978).

Practicing the habits of Jesus means influencing the lives of others with what He is teaching you. This week, call a woman you know who is interested in growing in her faith walk and tell her what God is teaching you in the area of spiritual habits. Be vulnerable about your own failures in seeking to "go deeper" in your relationship with Christ. Ask her how you can pray for her. Provide her with a helpful book or article that will give her greater understanding of a specific Christian habit.

> *May our daily lives be the bright and blessed proof that the hidden power dwells within, preparing us for the glory to be revealed.*
>
> —ANDREW MURRAY[8]

NOTES

Introduction: *Wanted: Real Christian Women*
1. Paraphrased from Margery Williams, *The Velveteen Rabbit*, quoted by Brenda Waggoner, *The Velveteen Woman* (Colorado Springs, CO: Chariot Victor Publishing, 1999), p. 11.

Chapter 1: *Develop a Passion for Jesus*
1. Carole Mayhall, *Come Walk With Me* (Colorado Springs, CO: WaterBrook, 1997), pp. 20-21.
2. Barbara Johnson, "The Greatest Joy Is His Love," quoted in Judy Couchman, *One Holy Passion* (Colorado Springs, CO: WaterBrook, 1998), p. 5.
3. Bob Pierce, quoted by Henry T. Blackaby and Claude V. King, *Experiencing God* (Nashville, TN: Broadman & Holman, 1994), p. 154.
4. John Ortberg, *The Life You've Always Wanted* (Grand Rapids, MI: Zondervan, 1997), p. 35.

Chapter 2: *Recognize the Unparalled Value of God's Kingdom*
1. Mimi Wilson and Shelly Cook Volkhardt, *Holy Habits* (Colorado Springs, CO: NavPress, 1999), p. 191.
2. Dallas Willard, *Divine Conspiracy* (San Francisco, CA: HarperCollins, 1998), p. 25.
3. Henry Blackaby and Claude King, *Experiencing God* (Nashville, TN: Broadman & Holman, 1994), p. 38.
4. Thomas Kelly, quoted by John Ortberg, *The Life You've Always Wanted* (Grand Rapids, MI: Zondervan, 1997), p. 132.
5. Francis Schaeffer, *True Spirituality* (Wheaton, IL: Tyndale, 1971), p. 3.

Chapter 3: *Cultivate Honesty About Sin and Limitations*
1. Dietrich Bonhoeffer, quoted by John Ortberg, *The Life You've Always Wanted* (Grand Rapids, MI: Zondervan, 1997), p. 119.
2. George Barna, quoted by Lael Arrington, *Worldproofing Your Kids* (Wheaton, IL: Crossway Books, 1997), p. 48.
3. Arrington, p. 54.
4. Richard Foster, *Celebration of Discipline* (San Francisco, CA: Harper & Row, 1978), p. 137.

Chapter 4: *Focus on Integrity of Heart Above Outward Behavior*
1. John Ortberg, *The Life You've Always Wanted* (Grand Rapids, MI: Zondervan, 1997), p. 202.
2. Harry Hein, quoted by Charles Swindoll, *The Tale of the Tardy Oxcart* (Nashville, TN: Word, 1998), p. 42.
3. Ortberg, p. 39.
4. Joseph Bayly, quoted by Swindoll, p. 286.
5. Francis Schaeffer, *True Spirituality* (Wheaton, IL: Tyndale, 1971), pp. 120, 122.

Chapter 5: *Think in Terms of Eternity, Not Time*
1. Ray C. Stedman, *Authentic Christianity* (Portland, OR: Multnomah Press, 1975), p. 125.
2. Jan Johnson, *Enjoying the Presence of God* (Colorado Springs, CO: NavPress, 1996), p. 70.
3. Anne Ortland, *The Gentle Ways of the Beautiful Woman* (New York: Inspirational Press, 1998), pp. 179, 178.
4. Corrie ten Boom, *Clippings From My Notebook* (Minneapolis, MN: World Wide Publications, 1982), p. 23.

5. William James, quoted by Charles R. Swindoll, *The Tale of the Tardy Oxcart* (Nashville, TN: Word, 1998), p. 571.
6. C. S. Lewis, quoted by Lloyd Cory, *Quotable Quotations* (Wheaton, IL: Victor, 1985), p. 118.

Chapter 6: *Practice the Life Habits Jesus Practiced*

1. Kay Arthur, "Quiet Time Alone with God," quoted in Judy Couchman, *One Holy Passion* (Colorado Springs, CO: WaterBrook, 1998), pp. 44-45.
2. Carol Kent, *Becoming a Woman of Influence* (Colorado Springs, CO: NavPress, 1999), pp. 39-40.
3. Partially paraphrased from *New Webster's Dictionary and Thesaurus of the English Language* (Danbury, CT: Lexicon Publications, 1992), p. 497.
4. Edith Schaeffer, "The Meaning of Meditation," quoted in Couchman, p. 61.
5. John Ortberg, *The Life You've Always Wanted* (Grand Rapids, MI: Zondervan, 1997), p. 90.
6. Richard Foster, *Celebration of Discipline* (San Francisco, CA: Harper & Row, 1978), p. 138.
7. Foster, pp. 140, 148.
8. Andrew Murray, *Abide in Christ* (Fort Washington, PA: Christian Literature Crusade, 1968), p. 176.

THESE FIVE BOOKS REVEAL HOW YOU CAN MAKE A DIFFERENCE!

Six Basics of a Balanced Life

Not just more items on your to-do list, *Six Basics of a Balanced Life* will help you understand what's really important and demonstrate that it's *not* necessary to "do it all." Learn to balance your life's priorities by settling your heart as Carol Kent and Karen Lee-Thorp show how Jesus is our most perfect time manager.

Six Basics of a Balanced Life (Carol Kent and Karen Lee-Thorp) $6

Six Keys to Lasting Friendships

In today's busy world, the need for friendship is as strong as ever. Discover from Jesus how to build new relationships and strengthen the ones you already have.

Six Keys to Lasting Friendships (Carol Kent and Karen Lee-Thorp) $6

Six Steps to Clarify Your Calling

Learn to make your life count as God's quiet voice leads you into the calling He planned for you.

Six Steps to Clarify Your Calling (Carol Kent and Karen Lee-Thorp) $6

Six Secrets of a Confident Woman

Do you sometimes lack the confidence to make big decisions with relationships or take risks in career planning? Discover the courage and wisdom that come from replacing self-confidence with God-confidence.

Six Secrets of a Confident Woman (Carol Kent and Karen Lee-Thorp) $6

Six Choices That Will Change Your Life

Are you so buried under minor choices that you miss the ones that could make your life rich with meaning? Build confidence, hope, and courage as you discover the way Jesus made the choices that would change lives.

Six Choices That Will Change Your Life (Carol Kent and Karen Lee-Thorp) $6

Get your copies today at your local bookstore, visit our website at www.navpress.com, or call (800) 366-7788 and ask for offer **#6099** or a FREE catalog of NavPress products.

NAVPRESS
BRINGING TRUTH TO LIFE
www.navpress.com

Prices subject to change.